Healthy Eating
for Lower Cholesterol

Daniel Green   Catherine Collins RD

Healthy Eating for Lower Cholesterol

photography by Lis Parsons

Kyle Cathie Limited

To my daughter, Eleanor (Daniel Green)

For Allan, Sophie, Alex and the Blackmores (Catherine Collins)

High cholesterol is directly associated with cardiovascular disease, and new national guidelines for healthy cholesterol levels, recently revised to be more stringent, mean that a great many of us need to bring our cholesterol down. Whilst our doctors fill out hundreds of prescriptions for cholesterol-lowering drugs, healthy nutritional eating remains a proven and supremely effective way of managing our cholesterol levels in a natural way, and is surely the best place to start.

Today, we are presented with so much good lifestyle advice it can often be difficult to know what is essential or relevant to us personally. We are always moving on to the next lifestyle trend with little regard for the sound, long standing advice that, if we look properly, continues to stand us in good stead. However, this new publication is an example of the very best kind of advice; a book that you can keep coming back to in order to achieve both the best quality in cooking terms and discover what's best for your heart and soul.

Healthy Eating for Lower Cholesterol provides a thoroughly reliable source of medically approved health advice that is the best line of defence against cardiovascular disease that can affect us and our families in so many serious and unexpected ways. At H·E·A·R·T UK we specialise in the treatment of the genetic disorder Familial Hypercholesterolaemia or FH for short. This affects around 120,000 people in the UK population, who unless diagnosed are likely to suffer premature heart attacks and strokes in their thirties and forties. Even men in their twenties can die from a first attack, and although these tragic events can be prevented with correct diagnosis, treatment and lifestyle management, 100,000 people remain unaware of their inherited condition.

This book is therefore a must-read, as it helps us to understand the basics of cardiovascular disease, how and why it develops, the essential role of cholesterol in the disease process, how the 'bad' type of cholesterol differs from the 'good' and how we can manage to keep it and other risk factors under control.

I am delighted to champion *Healthy Eating for Lower Cholesterol*. I highly recommend it as a practical, healthy eating guide for the whole family that represents an investment in the future but requires no sacrifice at all… bon appetit.

Michael Livingston
Director - H·E·A·R·T UK

Introduction

Few of us ever pause to consider our heart and circulation, despite the crucial part that they play in enabling us to lead a full and active life. Often, it is only when we're running for a train or exercising at the gym that we become aware of just how hard our circulation is working to keep up with the extra demands imposed on it.

Statistics show that cardiovascular disease ('cardio' – heart; 'vascular' – blood vessel) remains the UK's biggest killer, claiming the life of one in five men, and one in six women; and nearly half of all deaths in Britain from coronary heart disease are due to high blood cholesterol levels. Background damage to blood vessels has already begun by the time we approach our late twenties (even though it may be another fifteen years or so before symptoms to declare themselves), but by taking steps to change our diet and lifestyle we can greatly influence the health of our heart and circulation.

Time for a change

The fact that you've picked up this book indicates that you may be interested in – or perhaps concerned about – your heart health, and the risk of circulatory disease. Perhaps a health check has shown a raised cholesterol level? Or you have had a wake-up call from seeing a friend or relative suffer a stroke or heart attack and the way in which it has affected their quality of life. Or you may simply have decided that it's time to address what goes on inside your body in order to maintain your current good health well into old age.

Whatever the reason for your interest, the information in *Healthy Eating for Lower Cholesterol* will help you to choose a healthier way of eating, and you will be amazed at the abundance of foods allowed. It's a very positive diet, which, together with Dan's recipes, will give you all the inspiration you need.

The cholesterol conundrum

Of all the substances that our body produces, cholesterol seems to hold the record for bad press. Yet, what people often tend to overlook is that cholesterol is essential for human life – so important, in fact, that the body makes its own supply so that it does not have to rely on dietary intake.

What exactly is cholesterol?

Cholesterol forms the basis of steroid hormones such as testosterone and progesterone (sex hormones), cortisol (for stress adaptation), and vitamin D (for healthy bones). It also helps to build and maintain healthy cell membranes, and the insulating sheath around nerve fibres which act like 'broadband', speeding nerve signals to and from the brain. Also, the liver uses cholesterol to make bile salts that help to digest food more effectively.

The majority of the cholesterol in our circulation is made by the body, mostly in the liver from saturated fat in the diet. The remainder comes from dietary sources – animal foods such as fatty meat, eggs, dairy foods, seafood, fish and poultry. The liver controls blood cholesterol levels, reducing the body's natural cholesterol production when cholesterol from the diet is available.

The Cholesterol Couriers

Cholesterol has to travel from the liver to wherever it is needed in the body, so transport via the circulation is inevitable. Cholesterol is too 'waxy' to dissolve in blood, so it is transported around the body in a number of tiny 'couriers', called lipoproteins. A blood cholesterol level reflects the amount of cholesterol transported by these lipoprotein couriers at the time of a blood test. In general, a high blood cholesterol level increases your risk of cardiovascular disease. However, some couriers are considered 'safer' than others, so the goal of cholesterol management is to lower the levels of unsafe couriers, whilst maintaining more stable forms of cholesterol transport.

Just as vehicles on the road vary in size, so do our cholesterol couriers. Unlike road traffic, however, each lipoprotein can be remodelled by the liver into another type, changing its composition in the process. So, whilst they may start out as very large, buoyant and rich in fat, they gradually shrink in size, becoming smaller, denser cholesterol couriers, carrying less fat.

LDL ('bad' cholesterol)

Low-density lipoprotein (LDL) is the main cholesterol courier in our circulation; it transports cholesterol and triglycerides (fats) from cells that produce more than they can use to cells and tissues in need. Around 70 per cent of our circulating cholesterol is carried by LDL couriers. They vary in size depending on their triglyceride and cholesterol content – in healthy individuals LDL carriers are large and relatively few in number; in contrast small, dense LDL carriers are strongly associated with heart and circulatory disease, possibly because their small size allows them to penetrate the artery walls. LDL cholesterol is often termed 'bad' cholesterol for this reason, but its level can be reduced by diet and lifestyle changes.

Other cholesterol couriers

In addition to LDL, there are other transport couriers for cholesterol. Chylomicron couriers transport cholesterol and dietary fat from the digestive tract to the liver, and very low-density lipoproteins (VLDLs) then haul triglycerides around the body for uptake by cells requiring fat, before returning to the liver for reprocessing into LDL couriers. VLDL couriers may be likened to manufacturers' lorries, delivering large quantities of goods (triglycerides) to a central warehouse for collection by the LDL couriers. Triglycerides are an independent risk factor for cardiovascular disease, often raised in people who are overweight, drink too much alcohol, or have Type 2 diabetes (see page 19). Controlling blood sugar, and reducing alcohol intake controls blood triglycerides.

HDL ('good' cholesterol)

The smallest lipoprotein, high-density lipoprotein (HDL), is made in the liver from the remains of LDL cholesterol. Unlike other cholesterol couriers, HDL offers a 'collection' rather than 'delivery' service, collecting surplus cholesterol and fat from cells, and returning them to the liver for processing and removal. HDL also has the ability to 'pull' cholesterol and fat from newly formed deposits on the artery walls, helping to maintain healthy arteries.

Once excess cholesterol has been returned to the liver, it can be converted into bile acids for transfer to the gallbladder, or it can be recycled into lipoprotein couriers again. Each day the liver produces up to 2g of cholesterol and 0.4g of bile salts, the latter to replenish losses from the bile salt pool. Reducing the recycling of bile salts is how cholesterol-lowering stanol and sterol esters (see page 34) and soluble fibre function (see page 24).

How can I check my cholesterol levels?

The only way to establish your exact cholesterol profile is by having a blood test – often called a lipid profile. Lipid is a collective term for fats in the blood, and a blood test can tell you how much cholesterol is present, and what type. A random blood test can measure total and HDL cholesterol levels. A fasting blood test (where you fast for at least 12 hours beforehand, drinking nothing but water) can measure LDL cholesterol and triglyceride levels in addition, giving a more comprehensive result.

Ideal cholesterol levels

The goal of cholesterol management is to reduce the risk of cardiovascular disease. To put this into some sort of context, a high cholesterol level alone is thought to be responsible for 46 per cent of all premature deaths from coronary heart disease in the UK. Population studies may suggest a ballpark value for cholesterol levels, but our own individual cholesterol level and risk of cardiovascular disease are tempered by our lifestyle and other health concerns, such as high blood pressure. The table below gives guideline levels for each of the cholesterol couriers for general health, but the more stringent goals (the 'optimal' levels) have been devised by the six leading societies dealing with cardiovascular disease in the UK. Both sets of values are relevant for the general population. If you also have diabetes, high blood pressure or rheumatoid arthritis, then the optimal rather than guideline values should be your goal.

How is cholesterol measured?

Cholesterol is measured in 'mmols', a measurement of cholesterol concentration in each litre of blood (mmol/L). This is a world standard unit for measuring cholesterol except in the USA, where the preferred measurement is the weight of cholesterol in each 100ml of blood (mg/dL). Ideal blood cholesterol levels are quoted in both measurements (see table).

A simple way to remember the desirable level of cholesterol couriers is that <u>H</u>DL should be High, <u>L</u>DL should be Low, and <u>V</u>LDL (akin to triglyceride level) should be Very Low!

Guideline cholesterol levels

Total cholesterol: 5 mmol/L
   (195mg/dL), or less
LDL cholesterol: 3 mmol/L
   (115mg/dL), or less
Triglycerides: 1.5 mmol/L (57mg/dL)
   or less
HDL cholesterol: above 0.9mmol/L
   (35mg/dL)

Optimal levels

Total cholesterol: 4 mmol/L
   (156mg/dL), or less
LDL cholesterol: 2 mmol/L (77mg/dL),
   or less
HDL cholesterol: above 1.5 mmol/L
   (58mg/dL)

The Artery Highways

In order for the couriers to be able to deliver their loads effectively and safely, they need a healthy system to travel by – i.e. the arteries, veins and capillaries. Research suggests that we should not consider our total and LDL cholesterol levels in isolation, but also how well our arteries are maintained. The health of our artery highways and their ability to resist damage are the focus of most new research into cardiovascular disease.

Our body works hard to keep our artery surfaces fully repaired and so less prone to damage. Arteries are made of three layers. A strong outer 'coat' surrounds a middle layer of muscles that allow the artery to widen or contract as needed to control our blood pressure. An inner layer of smooth, flat cells (called the 'endothelium') creates the 'non-stick' inner lining of the artery which makes for smooth blood flow. The endothelium protects the artery, repelling toxic substances and marshalling defences if the blood vessel becomes inflamed or damaged. 'Resurfacing' of damaged endothelium is achieved by the components of a healthy diet (see pages 20–33).

How a cholesterol plaque is formed

In much the same way that a lorry will sometimes hit a pothole in a road, causing it to shed some of its load, naturally occurring damage to the smooth endothelium surface can encourage circulating LDL to deposit cholesterol. This then burrows below the endothelium layer, settling onto the muscular middle layer of the artery. Less stable LDL couriers (for example, those carrying 'oxidised' cholesterol), are more likely to deposit their unstable cholesterol load.

At this early stage, HDL couriers travelling along the artery may notice the cholesterol deposit, and can collect it from the artery wall for return to the liver, thus preventing development of an atheroma (or plaque). If it is not collected, however, the deposit generates local inflammation *within* the artery wall, attracting the interest of passing white blood cells. These then enter the breach and successfully attack the cholesterol, but in so doing become entrapped beneath the artery surface, forming a foam-like deposit.

Finally, in a sort of damage-limitation exercise, the endothelium surface forms a protective fibrin cap, resealing the surface and entombing the cholesterol, white blood cells and other debris (collectively known as an atheroma, or plaque) within the blood vessel wall. Remodelling of the fibrin 'cap' over the plaque eventually leads to a scar resistant to the natural 'stretch' of the artery wall. This hardening effect on the arteries is called atherosclerosis.

Over time, the atheroma increases in size. Initially it is accommodated by an outward bulge in the artery wall (called an 'aneurysm'). Eventually, however, the strong outer coat of the artery resists any further bulge, and the atheroma begins to push inwards, often rupturing the fibrin cap formed long ago to contain it. This has two possible outcomes. Either the rupture will attract red blood cells to form another clot to reseal, which can be dislodged into the circulation, eventually blocking a smaller blood vessel 'downstream'; or the ruptured plaque may shower atheroma debris into the circulation, with the same devastating outcome.

These are the principal mechanisms of a catastrophic heart attack or stroke occurring without warning, often resulting in major disability or death. Using ultrasound, it has been shown, frighteningly, that unstable plaque can rupture when as little as 20 per cent of a blood vessel is obstructed by an atheroma.

The effects on health of atherosclerosis

As well as cardiovascular catastrophies there are chronic symptoms associated with atherosclerosis, or hardening of the arteries, and these can compromise quality of life.

Angina is a pain across the chest, and sometimes the arms, shoulders or jaw, brought on by exercise. The extra demands made on the heart by exercise increase its need for oxygen, but 'furred' arteries have lost the ability to dilate, preventing the demands for additional blood to the heart muscle from being met. The resulting pain is the heart sustaining something similar to a 'stitch in the side', and relief is experienced only when exercise is stopped and the heart has restored its oxygen demands.

Peripheral vascular disease (PVD) is the obstruction (by atherosclerosis) of the large leg arteries. Failure to meet the metabolic demands of the legs and feet during walking can cause severe pain (termed intermittent claudication), hampering mobility.

Transient ischaemic attack (TIA) is caused by a temporary disturbance of blood supply to the brain. Transient ischaemic attack is often referred to as a 'mini-stroke' and is usually caused by a small blood clot blocking an artery in the brain, resulting in brief brain dysfunction and generally lasting for less than 24 hours before recovery is made TIAs are a warning of the potential for a more devastating stroke, so are treated seriously by doctors.

The cholesterol–circulation link

Since as far back as the 1950s it has been known that raised blood cholesterol – particularly LDL cholesterol – increases your risk of heart and circulatory disease. But until recently it has been unclear as to exactly why cardiovascular disease can occur in people with normal cholesterol levels.

That each developing plaque represents a tiny pocket of inflammation within the artery wall has helped researchers to prove that any inflammation in the body – obvious or not – will affect how robust the artery will be in terms of resisting damage.

Inflammation is now considered a major cause of damage to the endothelium surface, priming an inflammatory process that accelerates the rate of cholesterol deposition and, by extension, atherosclerosis. It has been shown that people with rheumatoid arthritis – a severe inflammatory condition – have twice the risk of death from cardiovascular disease when compared with the general population. Reducing inflammation within the body is, therefore, a prime target for cholesterol control.

Reducing Your Risk Factors

Medical research has helped to determine risk factors that identify those at high risk of cardiovascular disease. There are some factors that you can't change, including advancing age or a genetic predisposition; most, however, can be modified by changes in your diet or lifestyle.

In addition to a raised blood cholesterol, the following are all major causes of premature death from cardiovascular disease:

- lack of physical activity
- smoking
- obesity
- high blood pressure

And the more risk factors you have, the higher your risk of coronary heart disease.

Physical activity

Our modern lifestyle does little to encourage regular exercise, and many of us take no physical activity during a typical week. Individuals recording less than half an hour's physical activity a week are almost three times more likely to die in the short term than those who are more active.

Regular activity has proven positive health benefits, particularly for heart health. A single exercise session can beneficially reduce triglyceride levels by an average of 20 per cent, and raise HDL cholesterol by 10 per cent. Regular exercise leads to favourable changes in blood pressure, blood lipids, blood glucose, insulin and clotting factors. It also reduces the risk of circulatory disease, and slows the enlargement of any existing atheroma. What's more, the calories expended during regular exercise help with weight management, and increasing muscle tone improves blood sugar and cholesterol levels.

Fortunately, gym membership isn't required for this benefit! Thirty minutes a day of regular activity such as brisk walking, gardening, cycling, or dancing are all beneficial, but any exercise is

	FACTORS THAT INCREASE CHOLESTEROL LEVELS	FACTORS THAT INCREASE INFLAMMATION LEVELS
FACTORS YOU CAN'T CHANGE	▸ Increasing age and in particular being over 45 ▸ Being male ▸ Genetic predisposition to heart disease	▸ High blood levels of inflammatory blood proteins: homocysteine and C-reactive protein (CRP) ▸ Background inflammatory states, e.g. arthritis
FACTORS YOU CAN CHANGE	▸ Inactivity and a lack of exercise ▸ Smoking ▸ Obesity/being overweight ▸ High saturated fat intake ▸ High intake of trans fats ▸ Excess alcohol intake ▸ Uncontrolled stress and anger	▸ Smoking ▸ Obesity/being overweight ▸ High saturated fat intake ▸ High intake of trans fats ▸ High intake of plant-based polyunsaturates (omega-6) ▸ Poorly controlled diabetes ▸ High blood pressure ▸ Low or absent intake of omega-3 polyunsaturates ▸ Lack of anti-oxidant nutrients ▸ Excess alcohol intake ▸ Excessive iron intake

proven to be better than none. You should walk or exercise enough to leave you feeling warm and slightly out of breath. If you are unused to physical exertion, gradually build it up over several weeks.

Smoking

Smoking is a major cause of heart disease, other circulatory diseases and cancer, and there is no 'safe' level of usage. Smoking a pack of cigarettes a day doubles the risk of a heart attack.

The effects of smoking are three-fold. Nicotine constricts arteries, reducing blood supply to the heart and other tissues. Carbon monoxide from inhaled smoke reduces the amount of oxygen that can be carried in the bloodstream, and the combination of reduced oxygen delivery from reduced blood supply can damage the heart and other tissues. Nicotine and free radicals released from inhaled smoke damage the endothelium, initiating and accelerating atherosclerosis. Smoking also increases the levels of blood-clotting proteins, increases blood pressure and lowers levels of 'good' HDL cholesterol – a combination that is damaging to the heart and other tissues.

To continue smoking removes any health benefits possible from other advice in this book. Take advantage of 'stop smoking' campaigns to save your health.

Obesity

Obesity is an increasing health risk in the Western world. Most adults are overweight, and obesity impacts significantly on good health. Obesity is associated with an increased risk of diabetes and hypertension (high blood pressure), which alone and together are associated with an accelerated rate of atherosclerosis.

Body fat is not inert, but generates biologically active substances (called adipokines) capable of increasing background inflammation, and accelerating atherosclerosis. Healthy people with a higher body weight have higher blood levels of protein markers of inflammation (such as C-reactive protein, or CRP), and a three-fold increased risk of heart disease – and this is the case whether or not blood cholesterol levels are raised.

Losing just 10 per cent of your body weight if you are overweight carries significant health benefits, reducing the release of adipokines from the diminished body fat stores. Crash dieting is not the answer, but following a healthy diet with modest calorie restriction (between 1400 and 1800 kcal a day) will result in weight loss. Every 0.5kg of fat contains the equivalent of 3500 kcal, so reducing calorie intake to 500 kcal a day below your body's energy needs (see box) will help you to lose 0.5kg of fat per week.

Apple or pear?

The area in which your body stores its excess fat can influence health risks. A 'pear' shape (in which excess fat is stored around the hips and thighs) carries a lower cardiovascular risk than an 'apple' shape (in which body fat is stored around the waist). 'Apples' have higher levels of background inflammation, easily measured using blood protein markers. They also are more likely to have insulin resistance (increasing the likelihood of diabetes), in tandem with a high blood pressure, cholesterol and triglycerides. A combination of obesity, insulin resistance and other factors is referred to as the 'metabolic syndrome'.

Waist measurements rather than weight alone more accurately identify whether people are at risk of heart disease. Test yourself by comparing your waist size with the guide on the following page, and measuring your waist midway distant from the lower rib and the hip bone. Your tape measure should cross the belly button, not swing low 'below the bulge' as your trouser waistband might.

Average energy needs of adults (UK recommendations) (taken from COMA Report, Dietary Reference Values, 1991)		
AGE	MEN: KCAL PER DAY	WOMEN: KCAL PER DAY
19–50 years	2550	1940
50–64 years	2380	1900
65–74 years	2330	1900
75+ years	2100	1810

Waist measurements

	IDEAL VALUE	INCREASED RISK – SHOULD NOT INCREASE WEIGHT FURTHER	SUBSTANTIAL RISK – SHOULD ACTIVELY TRY TO LOSE WEIGHT
Women	80cm or less	80cm or more	88cm or more
Men	94cm or less	94cm or more	102cm or more

Waist-to-hip ratio (WHR)

This ratio appears to be a more beneficial guide in identifying people at risk of cardiovascular disease across all weight ranges. Measure the widest part of your hips, then divide your waist measurement by your hip measurement. For example, if your waist is 80cm, and your hip size is 96cm, your WHR = 80÷96 = 0.83. An ideal value is 0.83 for women, and 0.90 for men. Any waist-to-hip ratio above these values is a strong predictor for cardiovascular disease.

Clothing sizes

Recent research in nutrition has shown that, in the absence of weighing scales or a tape measure, clothing sizes can be a useful marker for risk of cardiovascular disease. For men, a trouser waist size greater than 38 inches in UK/US sizing, or 97cm in European sizing, predicts a greatly increased risk of heart disease, high blood pressure and diabetes. For women, a size 18 or above (size 16 in the USA or 48 in Europe) carries similar health risks.

Diet

The main influence on cholesterol levels from our diet is the amount and type of fat that we consume (see pages 26–32), but other factors also play a part. A regular, modest alcohol intake appears to

have some cardioprotective benefits, helping your liver to form more of the beneficial HDL cholesterol. A high alcohol intake, however, will remove any such benefits because of its toxic effects on the liver. (See also page 32.)

Following the dietary advice in the next section will naturally increase your intake of dietary antioxidant nutrients to help protect your body against free-radical damage.

Stress

In moderation, mental and physical stress appear to be beneficial to the body. However, sustained high levels of stress injures blood vessels, promotes atherosclerosis, and increases circulating levels of the blood-clotting protein fibrinogen, more than doubling your risk of cardiovascular disease. The stress hormones cortisol and adrenalin are behind these changes. A person with an angry, hostile personality has a significantly increased risk of cardiovascular disease.

Diabetes

Diabetes is on the increase in the Western world, and it is estimated that for every person diagnosed with the condition, another remains undiagnosed.

Type I diabetes occurs when the body switches off insulin production. This type requires life-long control of blood sugar levels by injection of insulin. The most common type of diabetes in the UK is Type 2 diabetes, caused not by a lack of insulin, but by insulin resistance. In Type 2 diabetes, the body produces insulin, but its effect in clearing excessive blood sugar levels is compromised by 'resistance' of body cells to accept it. Type 2 diabetes is linked to obesity, particularly central obesity with extra weight around the waist. Losing weight improves insulin usage and blood sugar levels, and also reduces the increased risk of cardiovascular disease.

High blood pressure

Blood pressure is the force of blood pushing against the artery walls, and it is necessary to ensure that blood supply can reach every cell in the body. A blood pressure reading comprises two numbers, one appearing above the other: e.g., 120/80 (an ideal reading). The higher figure (120 in this case) is the systolic pressure, representing the surge in pressure generated with every heartbeat. The lower figure (80) represents the diastolic pressure – the background pressure of blood between heartbeats.

Blood pressure varies throughout the day, being lowest when you sleep and rising when you get up, or when you are exercising, nervous, or stressed. Transient rises in blood pressure are the body's way of adapting to its environment and are perfectly normal. However, if your blood pressure constantly measures 140/90 or higher, you have high blood pressure (also called hypertension). Left unmanaged, hypertension can cause the heart to enlarge as it needs to work harder. It can also accelerate damage to the arteries, facilitating the process of atherosclerosis (see page 14) and increasing the risk of cardiovascular disease and kidney damage.

High blood pressure should not be ignored, and can be controlled with a healthy diet, adopting the Mediterranean style of eating (see page 20) in tandem with reduced salt and alcohol intake. If you are overweight, losing 10 per cent of your body weight will help to lower blood pressure. Increasing physical activity levels and, if necessary, medication can also help to control the condition.

In a nutshell

So, to summarise, maintaining a healthy heart and circulation requires a two-pronged approach: control of cholesterol has a significant effect on health and, at the same time, addressing health, diet and lifestyle issues can help to reduce inflammation within the body, protecting the artery walls from damage.

Blood pressure readings

CLASSIFICATION	SYSTOLIC BLOOD PRESSURE (mmHg)*	DIASTOLIC BLOOD PRESSURE (mmHg)
Ideal	Less than 120	Less than 80
Normal	Less than 130	Less than 85
High normal (pre-hypertensive)	131–139	85–89
Hypertension	140 or above	90 or above

*mmHg = millimetres of mercury.

The Heart-healthy Diet

In the 1960s an ambitious medical trial was devised to compare diet, lifestyle and ongoing heart disease rates across seven countries, selected at the time for their recognised differences in heart disease rates. Led by Dr Ancel Keys, an eminent American physiologist, the results proved revolutionary, demonstrating a five- to tenfold difference in the rates of heart disease between populations.

The 'Seven Countries Study', as it became known, provided evidence that a diet abundant in vegetables, fruit, pasta, bread and olive oil, and sparing with meat, eggs, butter and full-fat dairy products, reduced the occurrence of heart disease. It also highlighted that it was the type rather than the amount of dietary fat that had an effect. A higher intake of olive oil and omega-3 polyunsaturates from oily fish appeared to reduce the risk of heart disease and cancer. The population of Crete had the lowest rate of death from heart disease, and the longest life expectancy of all the countries studied, hence this healthful diet became known simply as the 'Mediterranean diet'.

Of course, there is not just one Mediterranean diet, since the countries surrounding the Mediterranean – from Africa to Europe – incorporate many cultural and food differences. Yet despite this, there are also many similarities, including an emphasis on plant-based foods (vegetables, fruit, legumes and wholegrains), along with a relatively low consumption of meat, a moderate intake of low-fat dairy products, modest alcohol intake, and a relatively high intake of olive oil.

Key aspects of the cardioprotective Mediterranean diet

▸ Abundance of vegetables, salads and fruit, rich in cardioprotective nutrients
▸ High in monounsaturated fats, such as extra virgin olive oil
▸ Balanced omega-3/omega-6 polyunsaturated fat ratio
▸ Emphasis on wholegrain breads and cereals, and legumes
▸ Moderate amounts of lean meat, fish, dairy foods and eggs
▸ Only a small amount of alcohol

There are two key nutritional approaches to reducing cardiovascular disease and maintaining good health. First, controlling the level and type of circulating cholesterol will minimise the risk of LDL cholesterol offloading into the artery wall. Second, reducing background inflammation in the body reduces the sensitivity of the endothelium, improving its ability to defend the artery against attack from blood cholesterol, blood sugar, or high blood pressure.

The Mediterranean diet deftly addresses both of these concerns, as well as aiding in the prevention and improved management of other chronic diseases such as high blood pressure, diabetes and cancer.

Being a whole diet, as opposed to so many others that concentrate on a specific factor, such as fat intake, for example, the Mediterranean diet has the edge for a number of reasons:

▸ The wide variety of foods makes it easy to follow – for lifelong benefit
▸ The high antioxidant content of the diet (being abundant in vegetables, fruit, and extra virgin olive oil) reduces heart disease and cancer risk, and can improve the symptoms and management of other chronic diseases
▸ It is a style of eating that can be adapted to different populations, tailored to local foods, but always maintaining the same health benefits. Many Asian countries, for example, have diets with a similar profile (sometimes termed MediterrAsian!) and also enjoy low rates of cardiovascular disease.

The next section expands on what makes a diet 'Mediterranean', and explains how certain foods can complement each other to enhance the health benefits. The closer you can make your diet to the Mediterranean model, the better your cholesterol control will be and, with it, the likelihood of healthy arteries.

Fruit and vegetables in the cardioprotective diet

'Eat more fruit and vegetables' is the simple yet profound health message that forms the cornerstone of the Mediterranean diet. A high vegetable and

fruit intake is common in healthy populations enjoying a low incidence of heart disease, stroke and cancer. Vegetables and fruit are nature's own 'functional foods', so powerful that the World Health Organisation recommends a daily intake of at least 400g a day – loosely translated as the 'five a day' with which most of us are now familiar. Fresh, frozen, tinned and dried fruits and vegetables and their juices all 'count' towards the daily five. Despite this, however, few of us manage even a scant three portions a day.

Nature's functional foods

Fruit and vegetables provide us with a host of plant substances that are essential for health. Phytochemicals (see right) and dietary fibres enhance their natural 'functionality' and their low calorie content offsets the calorie-rich Western diet that contributes to obesity. The average Mediterranean diet provides around 125 kcal per 100g of food eaten, compared with 160 kcal per 100g in the typical Western diet. Adopting this way of eating is a sure way to eat a lot more and weigh a lot less.

The antioxidants present in fruit and vegetables include vitamins, minerals and phytochemicals (plant chemicals). Vitamin C, beta carotene, vitamin E, zinc and selenium protect the body from damaging 'free radicals', natural by-products of oxygen metabolism within cells. Free radicals can be harnessed for useful purposes but a surplus can cause cell and tissue injury. Certain lifestyle aspects, such as smoking and excessive sun exposure, are also known to trigger excessive free-radical production.

Vitamins and minerals

Fruit and vegetables provide an abundance of vitamins and minerals – tiny nutrients essential for life and which support and protect the body in a myriad of ways. The B group vitamins, for example, help to release energy in the cells, protect against anaemia, and to maintain a healthy skin and nerve supply. Folic acid – a B vitamin found naturally in green leafy vegetables, oranges and pulses – works with vitamins B6 and B12 to reduce blood levels of homocysteine (a toxic by-product of protein metabolism known to cause damage to the endothelium and increase the risk of heart disease and stroke).

Phytochemicals

Plants contain hundreds of non-nutrient substances called 'phytochemicals' that provide the wide range of colours and flavours present in fruit and vegetables. As each colour supplies a different class of phytochemical, it is important to ensure that your diet includes an assortment

What counts as a five-a-day portion?

The servings below should give you an idea of what comprises a 'portion':
1 apple, pear or banana
1 handful of grapes, strawberries or cherries
2 tomatoes, plums or satsumas
1 large slice of melon
150ml fruit juice
1 tablespoon dried fruit/3 dried apricots
1 dessert bowl mixed salad
2 tablespoons cooked vegetables

Notes: Potatoes do not 'count' as a portion and each item can 'count' only once, irrespective of the amount eaten – it is the blend of colours and flavours that gives synergism to the plant-chemical benefits (so eating two or more apples, for example, is therefore just more of the same). (See also Phytochemicals above.)

of colours in order to enhance the usefulness of the fruit and vegetables you are eating. The UK Stroke Association's prevention campaign 'Eat a Rainbow' highlights this approach.

The importance of phytochemicals in providing additional health benefits beyond those of vitamin and mineral intake is increasingly recognised. Many possess powerful antioxidant abilities which are far greater than the effects of established antioxidant nutrients such as vitamin C. For example, lutein helps to protect the eye retina from UV light damage and lycopene protects against prostate cancer. Beta-carotene (derived from foods, not from high-dose supplements) seems to have protective properties against cancer, in tandem with vitamin C and E intake.

Flavonoids such as quercetin enhance vitamin C function, and catechins (found in tea) provide a substantial antioxidant load. Cocoa flavonoids have cardiovascular benefit, reducing LDL cholesterol, blood stickiness and background inflammation. So two squares of dark chocolate daily with a minimum 70 per cent cocoa solid content provide a substantial flavonoid load without excessive calorie or fat intake. The range of colours in extra virgin olive oil reflects its polyphenol content, providing antioxidant benefits. The deeper the colour (green or yellow), the higher the polyphenol content. Paler coloured, refined oilve oils lack the polyphenol content.

Where to find your phytochemicals

ANTIOXIDANT PHYTOCHEMICALS:	FOUND IN:
Lutein (carotenoid)	Corn, spinach, kale, E161b food colouring
Lycopene (carotenoid)	Tomatoes, watermelons, pink grapefruit, papayas, rosehips
Beta-carotene	Carrots, tomatoes, peppers, pumpkins
Anthocyanins	Aubergines, cherries, red grapes, blackberries, blackcurrants, bilberries, red cabbages, E163 food colouring
Quercetin	Citrus fruits, green and black tea, onions, apples, broccoli
Catechins	Tea, chocolate, apples

Fat and calorie content of nuts and seeds*

NUTS	G FAT PER 100G	KCAL PER 100G
Chestnuts	3g	170 kcal
Sunflower seeds	48g	581 kcal
Peanuts	50g	589 kcal
Cashews	48g	573 kcal
Pistachios	55g	601 kcal
Almonds	57g	621 kcal
Sesame seeds	58g	598 kcal
Brazil nuts	68g	682 kcal
Walnuts	69g	688 kcal

*All values given are for an edible portion, not including shells.

Nuts

Frequent nut consumption appears to offer some protection against heart disease. Diets supplemented with nuts, particularly almonds and walnuts, show a beneficial reduction in LDL cholesterol and total cholesterol, and a significant reduction in coronary heart disease risk. Regular nut and seed consumption (around 142g per week) reduces the levels of inflammatory proteins, indicating that nuts and seeds can help

Five ways to 'five-a-day'*

1 Enjoy a glass or 200ml carton of fruit juice every day, or try a mini 'health' drink (shot-size health drinks, available at supermarkets).

2 Always have a piece of fruit with your lunch and choose fresh or dried fruit for a healthy between-meal snack.

3 Include a side salad as a starter or side dish and cook an extra portion of vegetables – fresh or frozen – to eat with dinner. Have a 'stir-fry' meal once a week.

4 Try beans, peas and pulses for a non-meat meal at least twice a week. They lend themselves to the flavours of olive oil and vegetables such as onions, garlic, tomatoes, aubergines and herbs.

5 Nuts and seeds are easily added – as a breakfast cereal 'topper', to salads, or in seed and nut snack bars – but are best avoided if you are trying to lose weight!

* Note: Fresh, frozen, dried, tinned or juice all count towards the five a day.

protect against arterial damage. Nuts also provide protein, magnesium, copper, vitamin E, folic acid, fibre, potassium and the essential fatty acid alpha-linolenic acid (particularly walnuts). Nuts are high in fats, but mainly in the heart-healthy unsaturated fats. The one exception is coconut – this is high in saturated fat, although it is a different type from the animal-based equivalent. The jury is still out as to whether or not coconut oil is a health risk.

Legumes

Pulses such as peas, beans and lentils are excellent sources of insoluble fibre (roughage) and cholesterol-lowering soluble fibre. They are also rich in cardio-protective nutrients such as vitamin E, B vitamins, folic acid, calcium, iron and zinc. They are naturally low in fat and are a useful source of protein that can replace or extend meat or fish dishes. Dried pulses require initial soaking followed by prolonged cooking in accordance with their label so as to remove natural toxins. Tinned beans and pulses contain the same nutritional benefits.

The 'gel'-type soluble fibre found in pulses and porridge oats can bind not only dietary cholesterol, but a proportion of cholesterol-containing bile salts, preventing re-uptake for recycling by the liver, and therefore beneficially depleting the body cholesterol 'pool'. Further along the bowel, soluble fibres can act as a natural fuel source for friendly bacteria, helping to maintain a healthy bowel.

Soya beans

Soya beans deserve a special mention for their established health benefits, particularly in relation to heart disease, cancer, osteoporosis and women's health. Traditional soya foods include soya beans, miso, soya milk and oil, margarine, soy sauce, tempeh, tofu and tofu products. Soya protein concentrates, soya protein isolates and textured vegetable protein (TVP) are more modern ways of including soya in the diet.

A daily intake of 25g of soya protein can reduce LDL cholesterol by 10 per cent, sufficient to permit a UK health claim on foods that provide more than 5g of soya protein per serving. In practice, non-vegetarians often find 25g of soya protein daily difficult to achieve. For example, one soya yogurt provides 5g of soya protein, and 250ml of soya milk provides around 10g of soya protein. The benefits of soya protein appear to be dose-related – lower intakes having a lesser effect on blood cholesterol.

Not everyone appears to gain from soya protein. Research has shown that to receive the cholesterol-lowering benefits requires the ability to convert soya phytochemicals (called isoflavones) into a weak oestrogen called equol. It is this tandem effect – soya protein plus equol – that lowers LDL cholesterol. A third or more of the population lacks the facility to convert isoflavones to equol, and so do not benefit from its inclusion. It is not possible to predict whether or not you can produce equol. However, like all